Every Day Is
Earth Day

Every Day Is Earth Day

A Craft Book
by Kathy Ross

Illustrated by Sharon Lane Holm

Holiday Crafts for Kids
The Millbrook Press
Brookfield, Connecticut

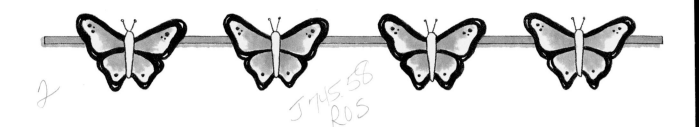

To Greyson and Allison—K.R.
To Michael—S.L.H.

Library of Congress Cataloging-in-Publication Data
Ross, Kathy (Katharine Reynolds), 1948-
Every Day Is Earth Day / by Kathy Ross;
illustrated by Sharon Lane Holm.
p. cm. —(Holiday crafts for Kids)
Presents 20 simple Earth Day related crafts that
young children can make from everyday materials.
ISBN 1-56294-490-8 (lib. bdg.) ISBN 1-56294-888-1 (pbk.)
1. Handicraft—Juvenile literature.
2. Recycling (Waste, etc.)—Juvenile literature.
3. Earth Day—Juvenile literature.
[1. Handicraft. 2. Recycling (Waste) 3. Earth Day.]
I. Holm, Sharon Lane, ill. II. Title. III. Series.
TT160.R714 1995
745.58'4—dc20 94-9835 CIP AC

Published by The Millbrook Press
2 Old New Milford Road
Brookfield, Connecticut 06804

Contents

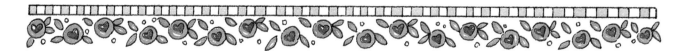

Celebrate Earth Day!

Earth Day is celebrated on April 22 each year. The first Earth Day was held in 1970 and was celebrated by schools and communities. Special programs informed people of the problems that our planet was facing.

Today Earth Day is celebrated with both education and action. Many people use Earth Day as a time to clean up public places and to plant trees and flowers. It is important to remember that the kinds of things we can do to help keep our planet healthy are things that need to be done all year. That is why the Earth Day motto is "Make Every Day Earth Day."

We need to recycle things so we stop creating so much trash. We need to stop wasting our natural resources, and we need to protect the living space of our vanishing wild animals. We need to stop polluting our air, land, and water and to work hard to clean up those places that are already polluted. Earth Day is a good time to learn about the many things we can do to help Earth be a healthy place for all living things.

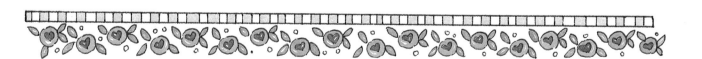

Scrap Paper Scratch Pad

We need to recycle or reuse things so that we
do not cover our Earth with trash.

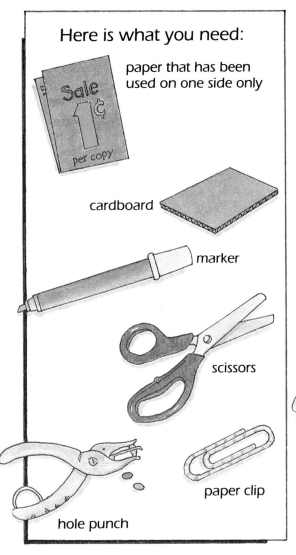

Here is what you need:

paper that has been
used on one side only

cardboard

marker

scissors

hole punch

paper clip

Here is what you do:

1. Save paper that has been
used on one side only.
When you have about twenty
pieces you are ready to make a
scratch pad. Draw a simple pine
tree shape on cardboard and cut
it out to use as a pattern. Trace
the pattern onto a piece of scrap
paper. Stack about five sheets
together and cut out the tree
shape. Repeat this step until you
have at least twenty trees for the
pages of your scratch pad.

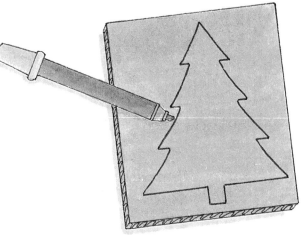

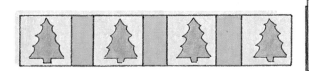
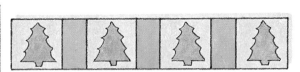

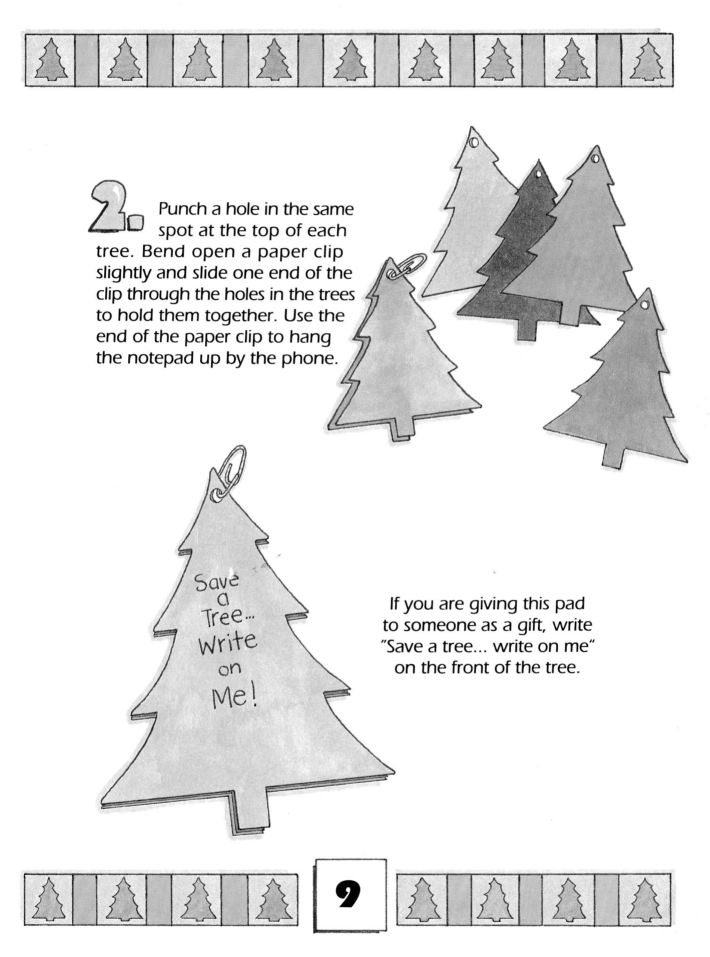

2. Punch a hole in the same spot at the top of each tree. Bend open a paper clip slightly and slide one end of the clip through the holes in the trees to hold them together. Use the end of the paper clip to hang the notepad up by the phone.

Save a Tree... Write on Me!

If you are giving this pad to someone as a gift, write "Save a tree... write on me" on the front of the tree.

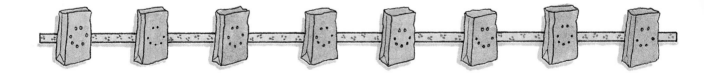

Trash Monster

We need to keep our land clean.

Here is what you need:

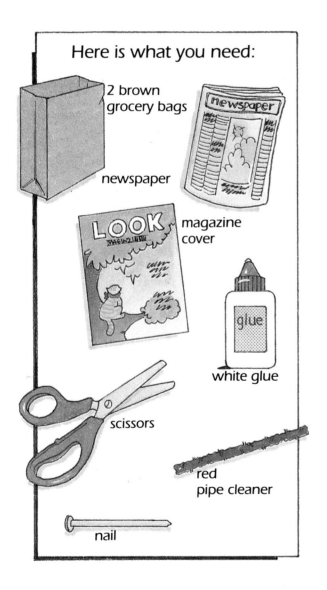

2 brown grocery bags

newspaper

magazine cover

white glue

scissors

red pipe cleaner

nail

Here is what you do:

1. Cut a large oval hole out of the bottom of a grocery bag. Open a second grocery bag and slide the first bag inside it so that the bottom with the hole is at the top. The hole is the monster's mouth.

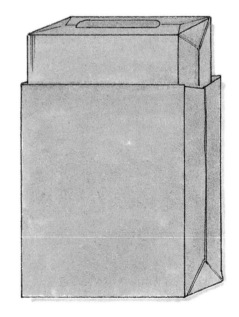

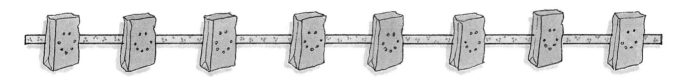

2. Crumple newspaper into balls and glue them above the mouth for eyes. Cut sharp teeth from an old magazine cover and glue them around the inside of the mouth.

3. Cut letters from newspaper ads to spell out "trash monster" and glue them on the front of the bag.

4. Poke holes through the top and back side of the trash monster with a nail, and string a pipe cleaner through. Twist the two ends together to make a handle.

Take your trash monster for a walk and feed it trash you find along the way.

Good Earth Necklace

We need good dirt to grow the plants
and trees we need to live.

Here is what you need:

clean dirt, such as packaged potting soil

white glue

cup and spoon

old plastic or china plate for drying

paintbrush

blue and green poster paint

clear nail polish

small paper clip

scissors

blue yarn

Here is what you do:

1. Use the cup and spoon to mix about two table-spoons of dirt with enough white glue to hold it together. Roll as much of the dirt mixture as you need to form a small ball for your necklace. Push one end of a paper clip into the ball to form a hanger. Wash the cup and spoon immediately. Let the ball dry on an old plate for several days until it is very hard.

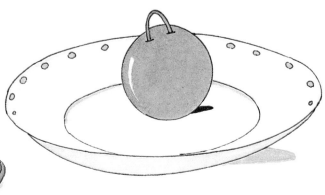

2. Paint the ball blue. When the blue paint has dried, paint on green land forms. Let the green paint dry.

3. Tie a long piece of blue yarn through the paper clip to make your necklace. Paint the ball with clear nail polish and hang it up to dry.

Remember to wash off your drying plate to save and use with other projects.

Giant Hand Flower

We need lots of healthy plants and trees
to make oxygen for us to breathe.

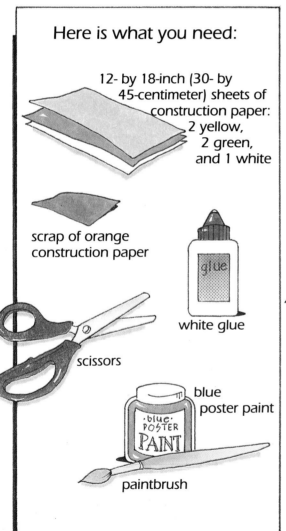

Here is what you need:

12- by 18-inch (30- by
45-centimeter) sheets of
construction paper:
2 yellow,
2 green,
and 1 white

scrap of orange
construction paper

white glue

scissors

blue
poster paint

paintbrush

Here is what you do:

1. Glue the two yellow sheets of paper together to form one long sheet.

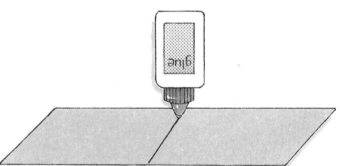

2. Cut a long stem and leaves from the green paper and glue them on the yellow paper.

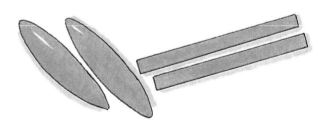

3. Cut a big flower shape from white paper and glue it to the top of the stem. Paint the palm and fingers of your hand blue and print hand shapes all around the flower for petals. You will need to repaint your hand for each petal to get clear prints. Cut a center for your flower from orange paper and glue it in place.

You can make a whole garden of flowers using different color combinations. Plant some real ones, too.

Seedling Necklace

A fun way to watch a seed sprout is to carry
it with you on a necklace.

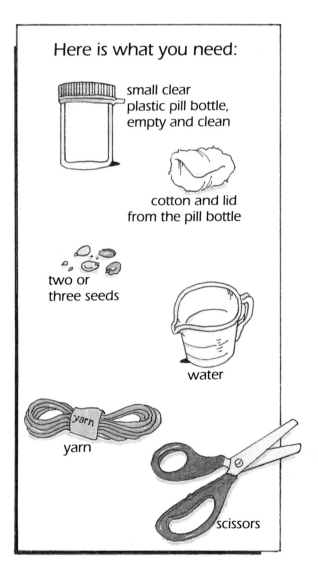

Here is what you need:

small clear
plastic pill bottle,
empty and clean

cotton and lid
from the pill bottle

two or
three seeds

water

yarn

scissors

Here is what you do:

1. Moisten the cotton saved from the bottle and squeeze it out. Put the wet cotton inside the bottle. Slip two or three seeds between the cotton and the wall of the bottle and put on the lid.

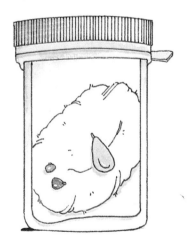

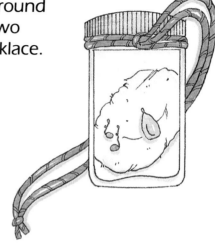

2. Tie a piece of yarn around the lid then tie the two ends together to form a necklace.

Wear your necklace until your seeds have sprouted. Then plant them in a flowerpot or in your garden.

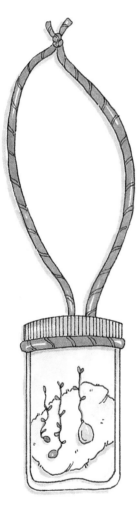

Anna's Seeds

Bag Saver

Don't throw plastic bags away. Use this box to save them so you can use them again and again.

Here is what you need:

large tissue box

brown poster paint

paintbrush

newspaper to work on

5 small green pom-poms

hole punch

scrap of yellow paper

white glue

2 small wiggle eyes

Here is what you do:

1. Stand the box on one end. Paint the sides and top brown, like the trunk of a tree. It will probably need two coats.

18

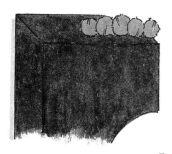

2. Glue five small pom-poms in a row on the top of your box, to look like a caterpillar. Glue two small wiggle eyes to the first pom-pom.

3. Punch four holes out of yellow paper and glue them on the back of the caterpillar.

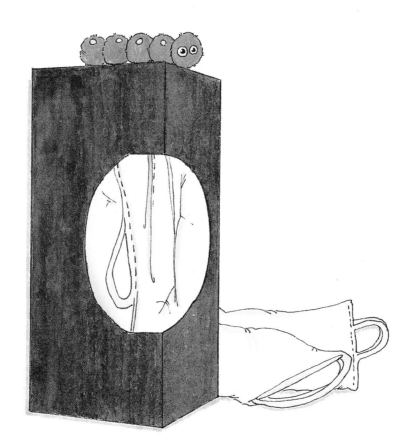

Puzzle Tree

Here's a fun way to recycle an old jigsaw puzzle that has some missing pieces.

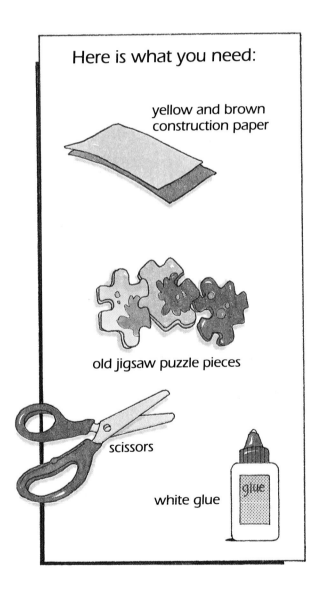

Here is what you need:

yellow and brown construction paper

old jigsaw puzzle pieces

scissors

white glue

Here is what you do:

1. Cut a tree shape from the brown construction paper. Glue the tree on the yellow paper.

2. Glue the puzzle pieces on the tree for leaves. If your puzzle pieces have lots of red, orange, and brown colors on them you can make an autumn tree and glue some of the pieces at the base of the tree, to make leaves on the ground. Pink pieces mixed in with light green pieces make pretty spring trees. Green pieces are just right for summer trees.

If your puzzle pieces are not the right color for the tree you want to make, just turn them over and paint them the colors you want your leaves to be.

Sock Cactus

Here is what you need:

two old white socks

sand

large detergent bottle cap

toothpicks

rubber band

green poster paint

·GREEN· POSTER PAINT

paintbrush

white glue

glue

Here is what you do:

1. Cut the foot off of a sock just after the heel. Stuff the part of the sock you cut off into the foot to make the cactus. You may need to put in part of another sock, too, to make it look full enough. Close off the sock with a rubber band. Trim off some of the extra sock if you need to, but be sure to leave about 3 inches (8 centimeters) for "planting" the cactus.

2. Paint the cactus green and let it dry.

3. Break several toothpicks in half, dip them in glue, and poke them into the cactus to make the spines. Let the glue dry.

4. To plant the cactus, mix white glue into sand. Use enough sand to fill the detergent bottle cap, and enough glue to moisten the sand completely. Stand the cactus in the cap and pack the sand into the cap around the cactus. The sand will dry hard overnight.

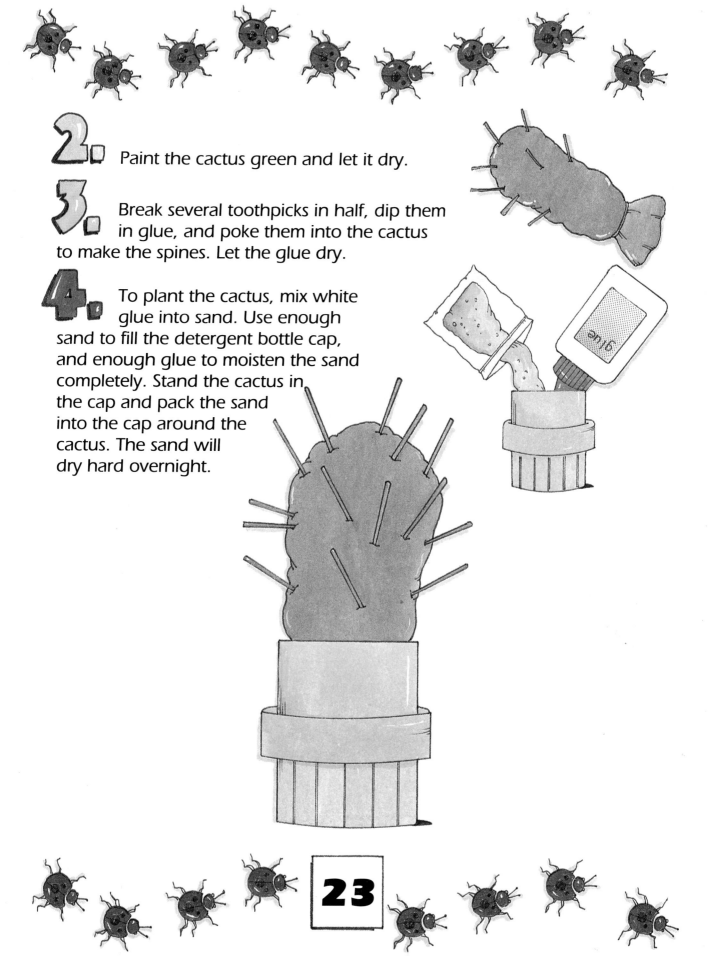

Recycled Wind Sock

We need clean, fresh air to breathe.

Here is what you need:

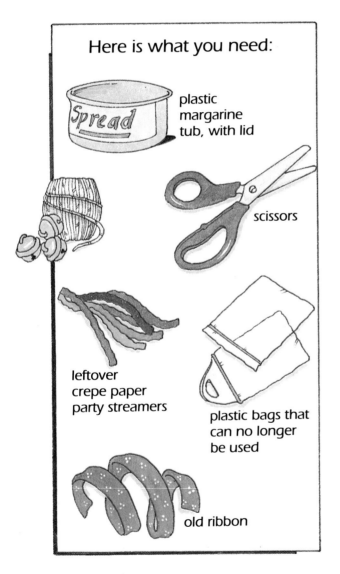

plastic margarine tub, with lid

scissors

leftover crepe paper party streamers

plastic bags that can no longer be used

old ribbon

Here is what you do:

1. Cut the bottom out of a margarine tub. Cut the center out of the lid, leaving the outer ring.

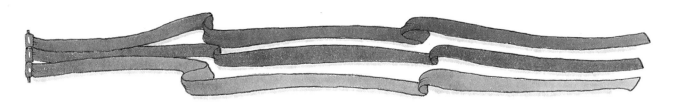

2. Cut 3-foot (1-meter) streamers from the crepe paper, ribbon, and plastic bags. Arrange them around the rim of the tub so that they hang down over the edge. Snap the lid over the rim of the tub to hold the streamers in place.

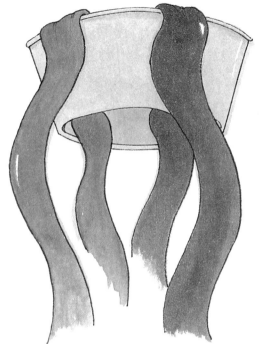

3. Tuck the two ends of a piece of ribbon under the lid so that it forms a hanger.

You can change or add to the streamers for your recycled wind sock as you find and save new things.

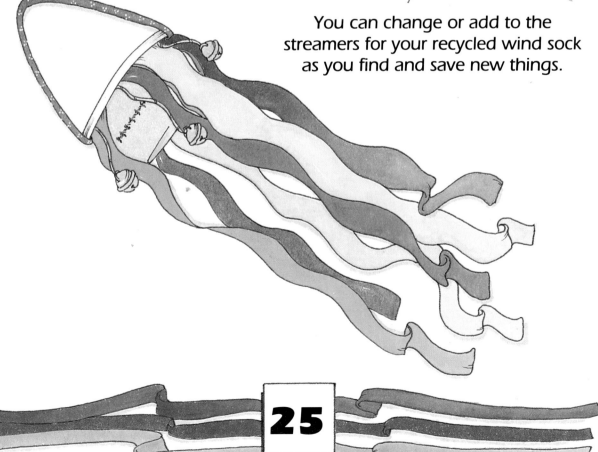

Egg Carton Bus

Less traffic means cleaner air. Using buses cuts down on air pollution.

Here is what you need:

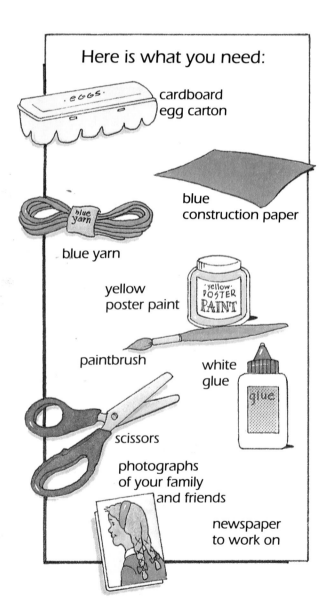

cardboard egg carton

blue construction paper

blue yarn

yellow poster paint

paintbrush

white glue

scissors

photographs of your family and friends

newspaper to work on

Here is what you do:

1. Paint the outside of a cardboard egg carton yellow and let it dry.

2. Open the carton up and cut a strip of blue paper to fit across the inside of the egg carton. Glue it in place.

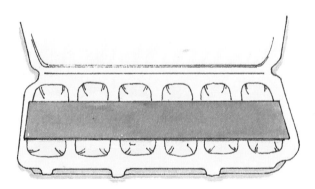

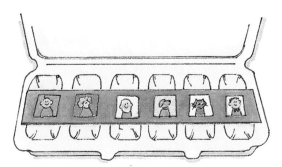

Close the carton and mark the strip at each place that there is an opening in the top of the carton. Open the carton again and glue photographs of yourself, friends and family on each of the marks so that when you close the carton it looks like they are looking out the windows of the bus.

 Cut wheels from blue paper and glue them on the front of the bus.

Cut a piece of blue yarn and string it through the top of the bus. Tie the two ends together to form a hanger.

The people in your bus can also be cut from magazines or the comics section of a newspaper.

Raindrop Mobile

We need clean water to drink.

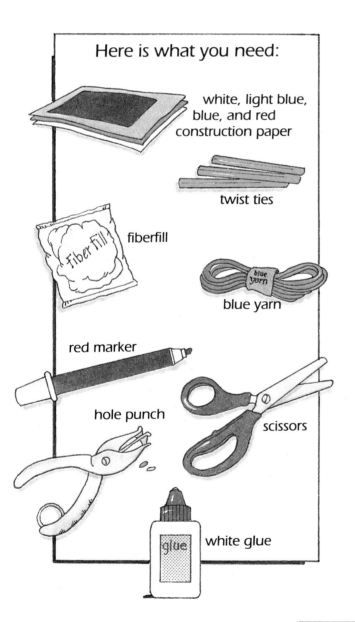

Here is what you need:

white, light blue, blue, and red construction paper

twist ties

fiberfill

blue yarn

red marker

hole punch

scissors

white glue

Here is what you do:

1. Fold a sheet of light blue construction paper in half. Cut three raindrops, each 3 to 4 inches (8 to 10 centimeters) high, from the folded paper so that each raindrop has a front and a back.

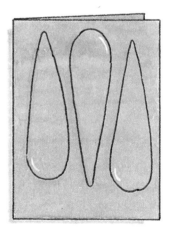

2. To make each raindrop, spread glue between the front and back pieces. Glue them together with four twist ties

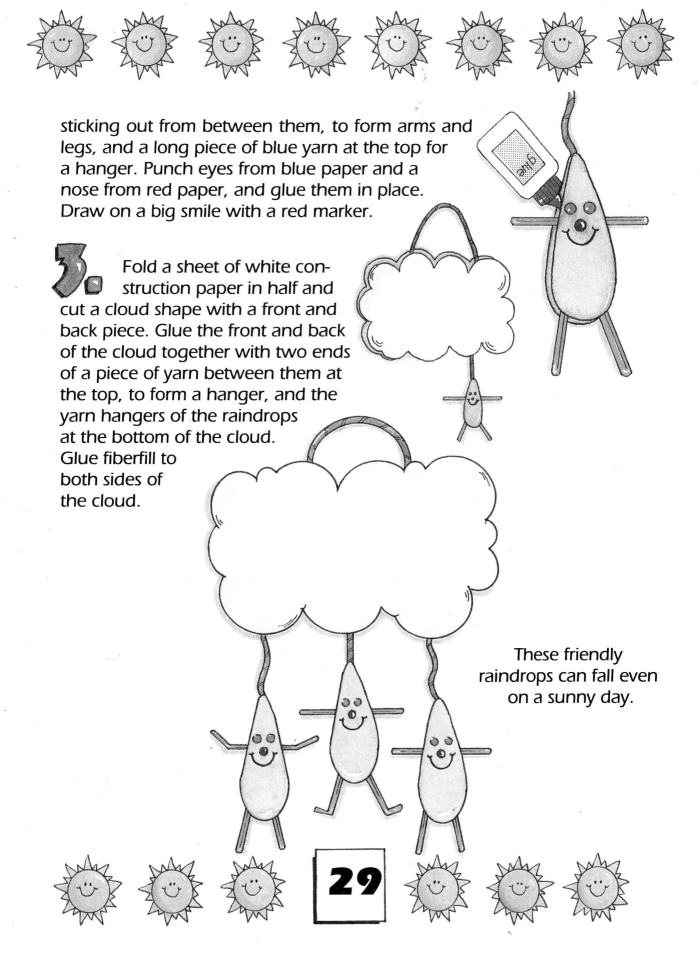

sticking out from between them, to form arms and legs, and a long piece of blue yarn at the top for a hanger. Punch eyes from blue paper and a nose from red paper, and glue them in place. Draw on a big smile with a red marker.

3. Fold a sheet of white construction paper in half and cut a cloud shape with a front and back piece. Glue the front and back of the cloud together with two ends of a piece of yarn between them at the top, to form a hanger, and the yarn hangers of the raindrops at the bottom of the cloud. Glue fiberfill to both sides of the cloud.

These friendly raindrops can fall even on a sunny day.

29

Oil Slick Paper

Oil will not mix with water. When it is spilled in our oceans it is a problem for both people and animals.

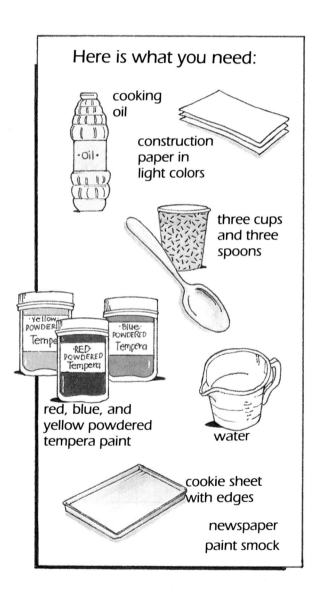

Here is what you need:

cooking oil

construction paper in light colors

three cups and three spoons

red, blue, and yellow powdered tempera paint

water

cookie sheet with edges

newspaper

paint smock

Here is what you do:

1. Spread out some newspaper to work on and to place your oily pictures on. Wear a paint smock to protect your clothing. Cover the bottom of a cookie sheet with water.

2. Pour about 1/4 cup of oil into each cup. Use about two tablespoons of powdered paint to color each cup of oil a different color. Mix each color well with a spoon.

3. Pour some of each color into the water in the pan. Swirl the colors together slightly with a spoon.

4. Carefully set a piece of paper down in the pan of water and colors. It will be ready to remove in just a few seconds. Pick it up at one end and let the excess water and oil run off. Then put it on a thick pad of newspaper to dry overnight. Each paper will be different as you stir the colors and add more oil and paint.

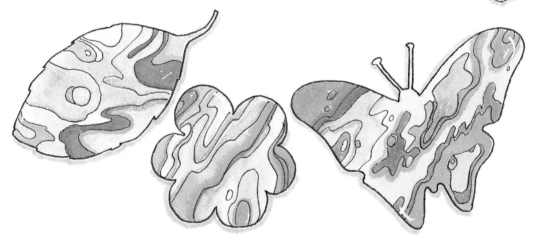

You can display your dried work as it is or cut it into pretty Earth Day shapes such as butterflies or flowers. Even when the paper is dry, it will be slightly oily, so it is best to display it taped to a window or another surface that can be wiped clean.

  **31**

Galápagos Tortoise

Damage to our Earth is making it hard for
many kinds of animals to survive. These animals
are called endangered species.

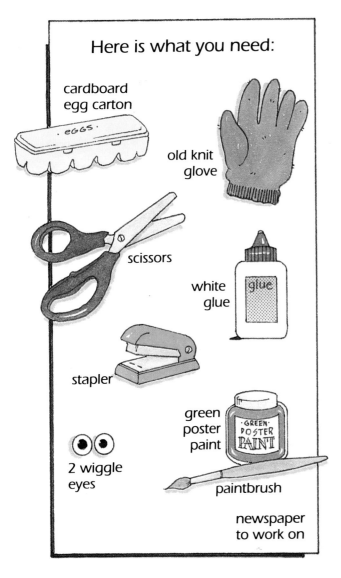

Here is what you need:

cardboard
egg carton

old knit
glove

scissors

white
glue

stapler

green
poster
paint

2 wiggle
eyes

paintbrush

newspaper
to work on

Here is what you do:

1. Cut the fingers and thumb off the knit glove. Cut the remaining hand portion into five pieces. Use the pieces to stuff the four fingers for the tortoise legs and the thumb for the head.

2. Cut a cup from the egg carton for the tortoise shell. Staple the head and legs in place around the shell.

Cut a second cup from the egg carton, trimming it so that it is slightly smaller than the first cup. Cover it with glue and push it up under the tortoise shell to hold the legs and head firmly in place.

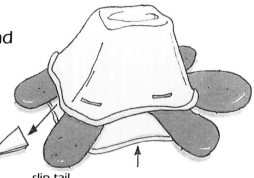

slip tail
between 2 egg cups

3. Cut a pointy tail from the lid of the egg carton and slip it in place between the two egg cups.

4. Paint the tortoise shell green. If you don't like the color of the glove you used for the head and legs you can paint them, too.

5. Glue two wiggle eyes on the head.

The San Diego Zoo worked to save the Galápagos tortoise from extinction. What else can you find out about this animal? What other animals are on the endangered species list?

Bird's Nest Supply Box

The birds around your house may not be on the endangered list, but they will be glad of the help you give them with this project.

Here is what you need:

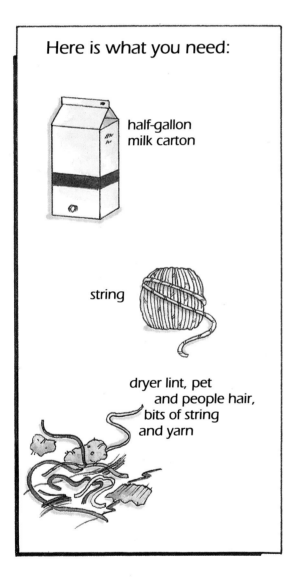

half-gallon milk carton

string

dryer lint, pet and people hair, bits of string and yarn

Here is what you do:

1. Ask a grownup to cut a flap in one side of the milk carton, using a sharp knife. The flap should extend halfway down the side. Fold it down to form a platform. Do the same thing on the opposite side.

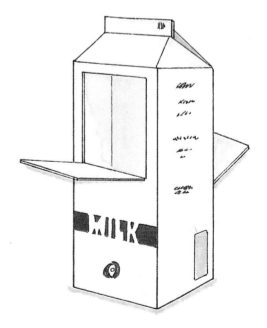

2. Thread a piece of string through the two openings in the milk carton and tie the ends together to form a hanger.

3. Fill the box with nesting material for the birds. Lint from the clothes dryer, hair, pet fur, and bits of yarn and string are all good choices. Hang the box from a tree branch outside.

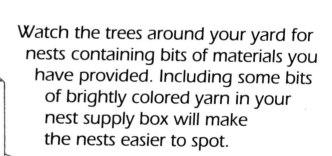

Watch the trees around your yard for nests containing bits of materials you have provided. Including some bits of brightly colored yarn in your nest supply box will make the nests easier to spot.

MILK

Summer Sun Rock

Different parts of the Earth have different climates. Some places have different seasons at different times of the year. Do this project outdoors on a warm, sunny day.

Here is what you need:

fist-size rock

old crayons

newspaper

small bag

Here is what you do:

1. Peel the wrappers off three or four old crayons. Lighter colors will work best. Put the crayons in a bag and smash them into small bits with your rock.

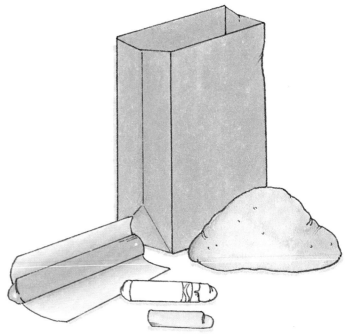

2. Put your rock in the hot sun on a piece of newspaper. Sprinkle the top of the rock with crayon bits and leave it until the crayons melt over the rock, coating it with colorful wax. Take the rock indoors so that the wax will cool and harden.

Use your pretty rock as a paperweight.

Changing Seasons Tree

Here is what you need:

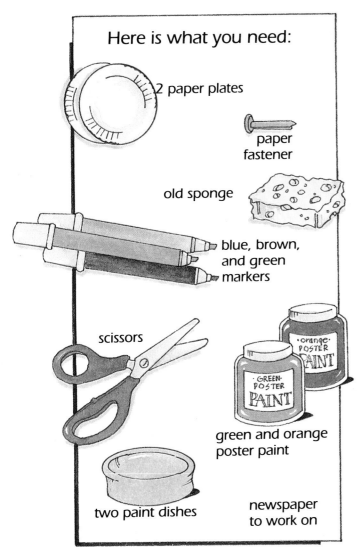

2 paper plates

paper fastener

old sponge

blue, brown, and green markers

scissors

green and orange poster paint

two paint dishes

newspaper to work on

Here is what you do:

1. Cut a half circle out of a paper plate, using the area just above the center of the plate. This will be the top of the tree. Use markers to draw a tree trunk, grass, and sky on the plate.

38

2. Pour the paints into dishes. Use a sponge to dab the paint on the second paper plate, to give it a leafy look. Use green on one half of the plate and orange on the other half, then let it dry.

3. Place the tree plate on top of the painted plate and hold them together with a paper fastener in the center. To make the tree turn from green to orange just turn the back plate around.

Leaves change color in the fall.

Winter Snowflake

Here is what you need:

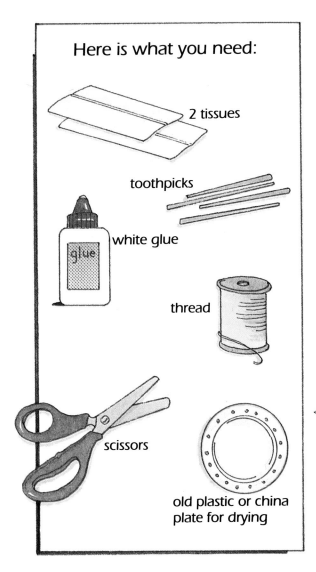

2 tissues

toothpicks

white glue

glue

thread

scissors

old plastic or china
plate for drying

Here is what you do:

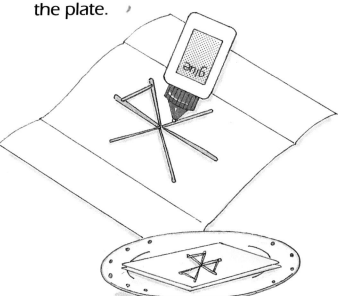

1. Open one tissue and place it on a smooth work surface. Make a snowflake design on the tissue using toothpicks covered with glue. Squeeze a small puddle of glue at the center of the snowflake to help hold it together. Cover the snowflake with another tissue. Let it dry flat on the plate.

40

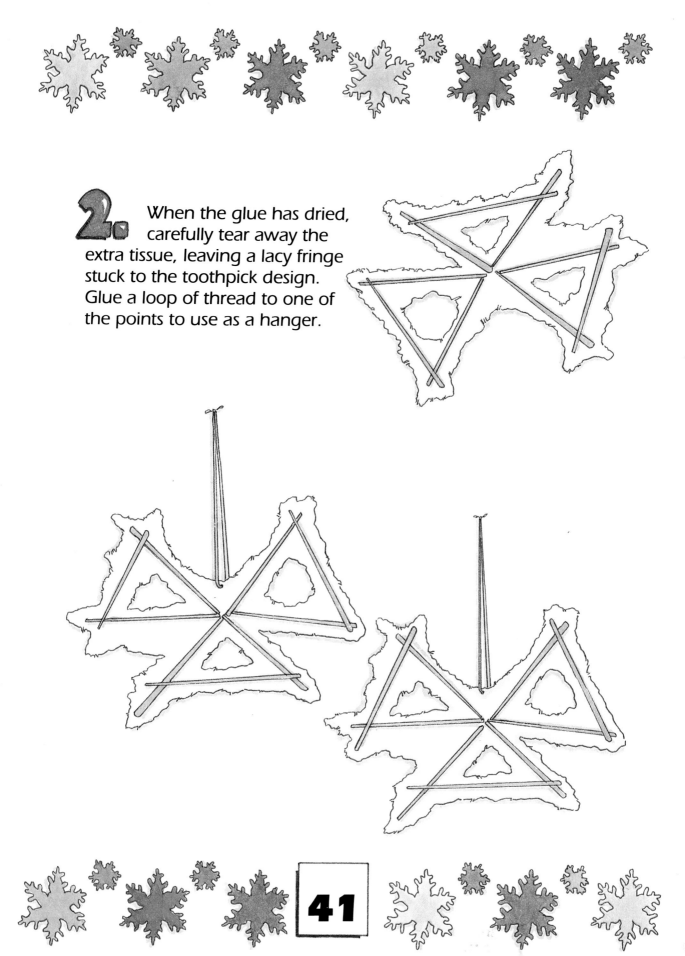

2. When the glue has dried, carefully tear away the extra tissue, leaving a lacy fringe stuck to the toothpick design. Glue a loop of thread to one of the points to use as a hanger.

Spring Showers to Flowers

Here is what you need:

2 paper plates

paper fastener

brown construction paper

flower pictures from a seed catalog or greeting cards

Seed Catalog
seeds
DAISY

blue and yellow poster paint

BLUE POSTER PAINT

YELLOW POSTER PAINT

paintbrush

silver glitter

white glue

scissors

Here is what you do:

1. Cut a scalloped line across one paper plate just below the middle of the plate to make an umbrella. Paint the umbrella yellow and let it dry. Cut a handle for it from brown paper and glue it in place.

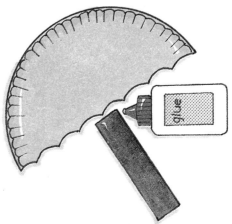

glue

2. Paint half the second paper plate blue and glue on pictures of flowers to cover the other half. Let the plate dry.

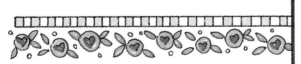

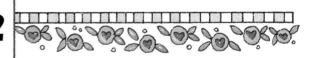

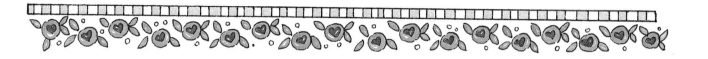

3. To make tiny raindrops on the blue side of the plate, put on spots of glue and sprinkle silver glitter over them. Let the glue dry.

4. Place the umbrella on top of the other plate and hold them together by pushing a paper fastener through the center of both plates. Turn the umbrella upside down to go from April showers to a basket of May flowers.

"April showers bring May flowers."

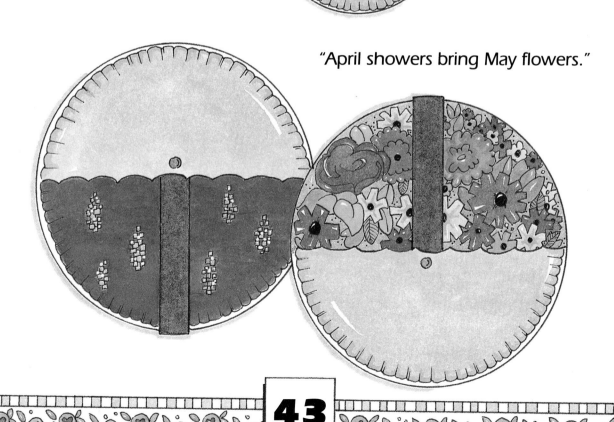

Earth Light Catcher

Here is what you need:

small plastic lid from a margarine tub

cup and spoon

white glue

paper clip

blue food coloring

blue yarn

scissors

brown permanent marker

Here is what you do:

1. Pour about one third of a cup of glue into a cup and color it with about five drops of blue food coloring. The glue will dry much darker than it looks wet, so do not use more than this.

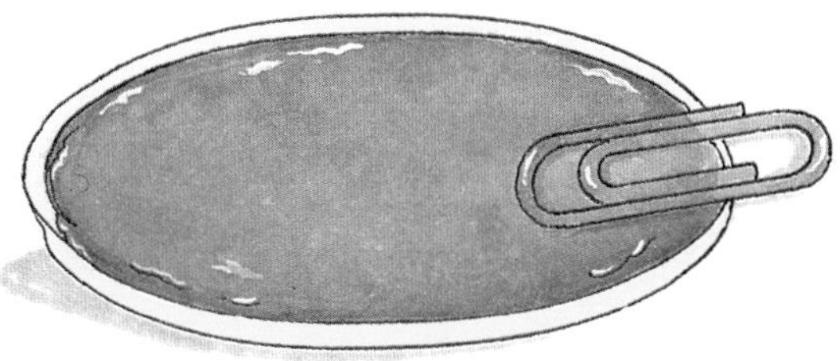

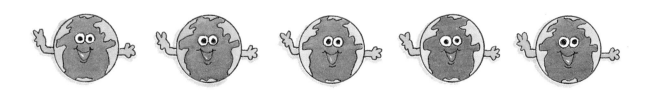

2. Fill the plastic lid with the colored glue and set a paper clip in the glue to use as a hanger. Wash the cup and spoon immediately. Let the glue dry completely. This could take up to a week.

3. When the glue is totally dry, peel the blue circle out of the lid. Use a brown permanent marker to draw on landforms.

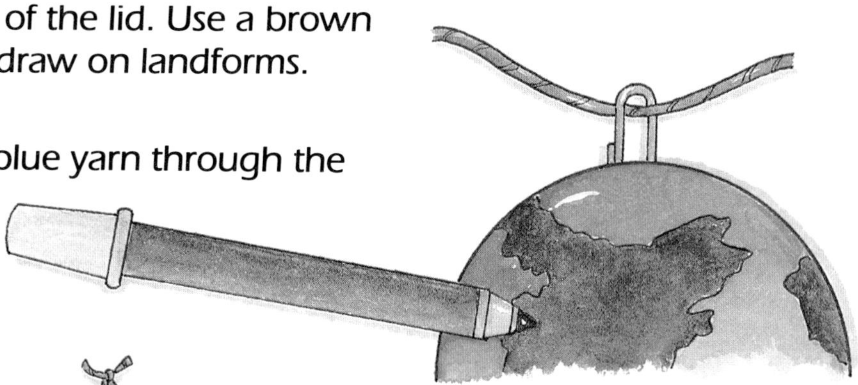

4. Tie a piece of blue yarn through the paper clip and hang the Earth in a sunny window.

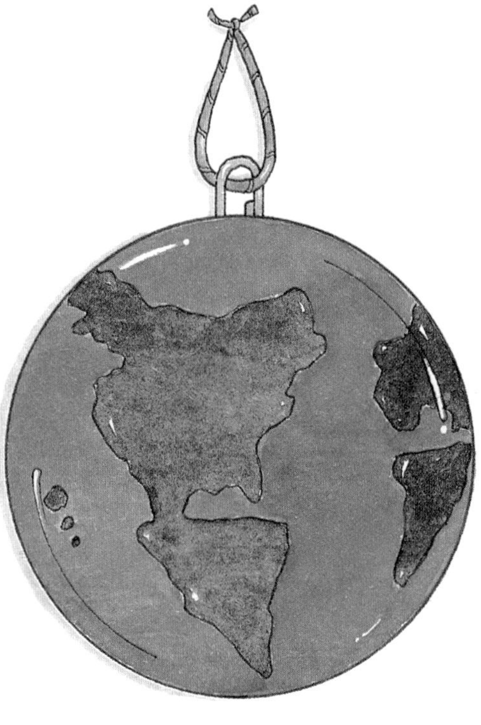

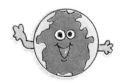

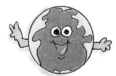

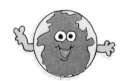

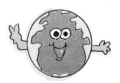

Talking Earth Puppet

If our Earth could talk, what do you think it would tell us?

Here is what you need:

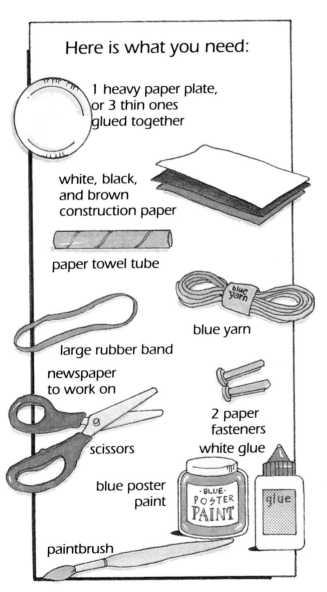

1 heavy paper plate, or 3 thin ones glued together

white, black, and brown construction paper

paper towel tube

blue yarn

large rubber band

newspaper to work on

scissors

2 paper fasteners

blue poster paint

white glue

paintbrush

Here is what you do:

1. Paint the bottom of the plate blue and let it dry.

2. Cut landforms from brown paper and glue them on the plate to make the Earth. Cut eyes from white and black paper and glue them in place. Poke the fasteners through the bottom of the plate far enough apart so that the rubber band will hook over each fastener to form the mouth of the puppet.

3. Tie a long piece of blue yarn to the bottom of the rubber band. Cut two slits in the top of a paper towel tube and slide the bottom of the Earth puppet into the slits so that you have a holder for the puppet. Drop the mouth string through the tube so that it hangs out the other end. To move the puppet's mouth just pull gently on the end of the yarn.

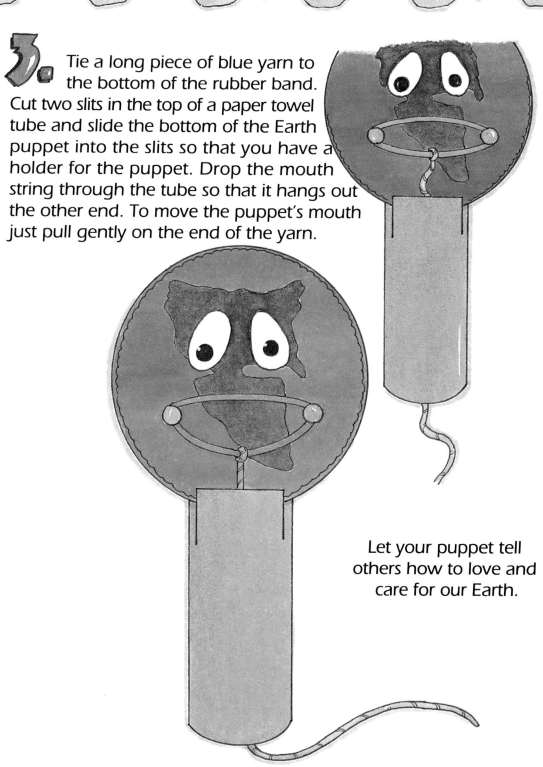

Let your puppet tell others how to love and care for our Earth.

About the author and illustrator

Twenty years as a teacher and director of nursery school programs have given Kathy Ross extensive experience in guiding young children through craft projects. Her craft projects have appeared in **Highlights** magazine, and she has also written numerous songs for young children. She lives in Oneida, New York.

Sharon Lane Holm won awards for her work in advertising design before shifting her concentration to children's books. Her illustrations have since added zest to books for both the trade and educational markets. She lives in New Fairfield, Connecticut.

DATE			